The Challenge
of Value

How to Drive Up the Value of your Products and Services and Make a Lot More Profit!

Harry Macdivitt & Mike Wilkinson
Axia Value Solutions Ltd

Published 2010 by arima publishing

www.arimapublishing.com

ISBN 978-1-84549-449-0

Printed and bound in the United Kingdom

Typeset in Century 12

abramis is an imprint of arima publishing

arima publishing
ASK House, Northgate Avenue
Bury St Edmunds, Suffolk IP32 6BB
t: (+44) 01284 700321

www.arimapublishing.com

Praise for The Challenge of Value...

"Macdivitt and Wilkinson, based on solid experience, address a fundamental issue in sales - how to understand, create and deliver value for the customer. Their easy-to-read book is a must for all new, aspiring and seasoned sales professionals."
Bill Donaldson, Professor of Marketing, Aberdeen Business School

"If you want to win in today's competitive marketplace, then you need to understand the concept of Value and how to apply it to your products and services. This book shows you how in a clear and concise way."
Jack Matton, Director of Sales Process Improvement, Alstom Power

"I really enjoyed reading the book and agree wholeheartedly with the message it conveys......an entertaining read and a useful primer for anyone that wants to know the basics of value based selling".
Ebi Zadeh Director - EIA Growth Implementation Services Frost & Sullivan

"The contents of this book are at the very heart of understanding value. As a result, I think it would be extremely helpful for readers wishing to understand and implement value in their own organisations".
Helmut Stiegler, Manager Sales & Marketing-Sales Excellence, Siemens Industry Automation Division

"Everyone who ever negotiates with anyone else about anything will find this book ... valuable! A very powerful and important message eloquently revealed"
Symon Vegro, Sector Head, Telefonica O2

"Far too little work has been done around the question of value, this is a notable contribution to the field. ...... This book will give you a head start in communicating the value inherent in your goods and services to the stakeholders who matter most to your business...your customers".
David Thorp, Director of Research and Professional Development, The Chartered Institute of Marketing

"The Challenge of Value is highly thought provoking and challenges the perception that 'value' means 'price' with some interesting and amusing examples. If you are interested in value there is enough here to allow you to take note of how you currently 'value' and 'price' products and how you could be missing revenue opportunities by undervaluing what your whole product offering gives."

Russell Connelly GSM Product Manager | Motorola Home & Networks Mobility

Table of Contents

Who are we?

Harry Macdivitt trains and consults on a wide range of marketing and business areas across the world. His passion is value and Value Based Pricing . He brings a wealth of experience in strategic marketing and management to his training – having worked in senior positions in sales, marketing and business development for the public sector, academic, manufacturing and services sectors.

Mike Wilkinson has worked worldwide with clients across a diverse range of business sectors and has experience of FMCG, as well as B2B sales. This experience has given him a unique perspective on the sales process and the ability to deal with sales issues from a practical perspective delivering effective new ways of working and building winning Value Propositions.

At **Axia Value Solutions** we help our clients to reach a deeper understanding of the value of the solutions they deliver to their customers and through that understanding enable them to differentiate, price and communicate their offer accordingly.

We would really like to hear from you about your experiences identifying, communicating and pricing your value. We would particularly like to hear from those with experience of implementing a Value Based Pricing approach – successfully or otherwise! So please contact us at info@axiavalue.com and visit the website at www.axiavalue.com

INTRODUCTION

So why this book......?
We have been lucky enough to deliver training programmes throughout the world on both value and value based pricing. We have been somewhat surprised at how little understanding there generally seems to be about value, what it is, why it's important, how it should be communicated and what its role is in determining pricing strategy.

On numerous occasions we've been asked to recommend books to delegates to help them better understand value, differentiation, value based pricing and the value proposition. This book isn't our way of saying there wasn't one we could recommend. It's just our way of responding to an opportunity when we see one!

Value is a vitally important concept in modern business. Its currency has been devalued because of a lack of clarity about its meaning and its constant use to denote lower price i.e. supermarkets' "Value" ranges.

A proper understanding of the meaning of value in a business context is very important if we are to defend our existing prices against attack or demonstrate why our products and/or services should command a premium price. Not only does this help us build a justifiable value based price, but it also helps us to develop an effective value proposition – the reason why the customer should choose us rather than a competitor.

When the customer rejects our offer, it is usually because they don't understand the real value of our offer to them, or because a competitor has worked harder to build their proposition. Salespeople cannot be blamed entirely for this. Ask a sales person why they lost the business and poor sales are usually blamed on price. More often than not, discounting (usually the completely wrong response) is the method used to resolve the problem. Poor selling skills often means that the correct decision makers never even get to hear the real value proposition.

In our experience, the problem rarely lies in the pricing methods. This, after all, is generally basic arithmetic. In almost every case, inadequate attention to value, and what this means to the buyer, lies at the heart of the issue.

Solve this, and the rest will follow.

There is a lot of evidence to suggest that the quickest and most effective way to impact bottom line results is to focus attention on pricing. However, most companies continue to focus on cost reduction. Why? Probably because slashing budgets and reducing spend is seen as quicker and easier than tackling customers about pricing - potentially contentious meetings with buyers and best avoided!. The real problem lies in an inability to identify true value and communicate that value to the people in the customers business who care.

A short book like this can only provide a useful introduction and we hope it stimulates your interest and encourages you to find out more about value generally and value based pricing in particular. They are becoming increasingly important. As buyers move away from accepting the old "features and benefits" approach and look towards a much more rigorous evaluation of their options, sellers must review and revise their own approach to meet this new challenge.

But remember, you cannot sell value to people who, frankly, don't care about value. You need to sell your value to the people for whom it matters. In our forthcoming Practitioner's Guide to Value Based Pricing we will be exploring these ideas in much greater detail.

......**Why now?**

We are probably facing, today, the most complex, fast-moving and competitive environment in the history of commerce. Our view is simple. The only way out is a clear, unambiguous and assertive managerial focus on value, driving value through all aspects of your business, from product development, differentiation, marketing communications, selling, pricing and building and delivering the value proposition.

In this short book we have crystallised lessons from a lifetime of experience in a volume you can read from cover to cover in an hour. A valuable way to spend an hour. A great way to change your business. Enjoy!

Who is it for?

This book is written primarily for:

a. everyone in business that is involved in delivering value to customers, and

b. those subsequently involved in determining what to charge for the products and services that the company provides.

In other words, everyone involved in business.

PART 1: The Challenge of Value

But they taste great......
I can remember my grandmother always used to say to my brother and me "You children know the value of nothing!" I thought at the time this was a little harsh. For instance, I knew just how many black jacks[1] I could get for a shilling. I knew they tasted great and altogether I thought they were fantastic value. My Grandmother thought they were cheap and disgusting and would rot my teeth.

She used to love sprouts and would insist we ate them as they were "a valuable addition to your diet". How could anyone say black jacks were disgusting and then try to persuade me to eat sprouts!

It just shows you how very different people's perceptions of value can be. But then value is only value when it is perceived as such – I thought black jacks tasted great and you got lots for your money. For me that was real value at the time.

---

[1] A delightful sweet/candy from my childhood!

My grandmother thought otherwise and used to ask me "why do you want to waste your money on those?"

But to me it wasn't waste – it was great value. Which brings us to value and what it is.

I can remember speaking at a conference in Copenhagen a few years ago. As part of the session I asked the group to define value, since this is what they had told me they provided to their customers. There were just over 100 people there, sat around tables of 10. On each of the tables I could see them beavering away at their definitions and I was immediately struck by the difficulty they were obviously having. I finally received about 10 cards, each with a definition written on it (each different as it turned out). It was something of a mixed bunch that more than demonstrated the difficulty they had been having. I had decided to read out each of the groups' ideas to the audience. About three quarters of the way through I turned over a card to find a definition that seemed to sum up the whole exercise. It had four words on it, the sum of the combined thinking of a group of senior people involved in selling big ticket contracts:

Value is a mystery

I didn't know quite what to say. The room went quiet. Unusually for me, I went quiet, at least just for a moment. But then it dawned on me that, together with all the other definitions the groups had come up with, that was exactly what value was...a mystery. And whilst value remained a mystery it would be impossible to sell on value. And it dawned on the

> .....they started out believing they were providing their customers with great value, but ended up recognising that they didn't actually know what value looked like...........

group as well. They had started out believing that they were providing their customers with great value, but ended by recognising that they didn't actually know what value looked like to themselves, let alone to their clients. So they'd better find out.

Following that conference, we have consistently found that there is the same or similar degrees of confusion about what constitutes value in many businesses. In these increasingly difficult times that is something of a serious problem and plays into the hands of those people who see value expressed purely through price.

If your only differentiation is price (and that is extremely unlikely) then your differentiation is transitory to say the least. The minute someone comes up with a lower price than yours your differentiation has gone, and so, quite possibly, has your business.

So where else can you look for value? The key starting point is in recognising that:

Value is defined by the client, not by you.

It doesn't matter one bit how wonderful you think the value is that you offer, if the client doesn't see it that way, then you aren't offering value – or at least not the value your client wants. Of course you will want to spend time thinking about your overall value proposition, the generic view of what you offer your clients, but this will then need to be tailored to the specific needs of the client with whom you are dealing. More on this a little later. However, you will only be able to do this if you can find out what it is that your client does value. So what kinds of thing are likely to be important?

One of the problems we have found is that not only do people have difficulty defining value, they also have difficulty in recognising its constituent parts. The instant answer is price, but price and value are simply not the same thing. Indeed, sometimes there is no obvious connection between the two at all.

For example, in 1999 Tracey Emin's soiled bed, My Bed, was sold to Charles Saatchi for £150, 000. Mr Saatchi clearly saw a value in the "artwork" that few others could see. To him the value was obviously worth the purchase price although, since I can't speak for him, I have no idea what that value is.

Even within a business, different people will have different views of the value of various products and services. Think about the differences of opinion that occur in your own firm when you are making significant purchase decisions. Then think about your suppliers and how, if they really understood the things that you, your colleagues and your business truly valued, they would be so much better positioned to deal with you. And then think how much better positioned you would be to deal with your clients if you really knew what they valued (and by really, I mean really, not just your best guess!) But the problem is, as the group in Copenhagen demonstrated, we can't define value!

We have developed an approach to understanding value called "The Value Triad©". It brings together the key elements of value into an understandable whole, whilst recognising that different people will have different views.

So think about value from your own firms perspective (or your own perspective) as we take a look at the three elements of:

"The Value Triad©".

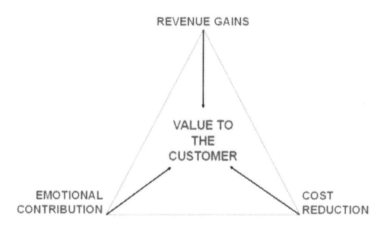

The first two elements are the logical, objective, measurable elements:

Revenue Gain. If you can show your customers or clients that your solution will deliver a quantifiable gain in revenue, then the chances are you are delivering the kind of value they are looking for. Revenue gain is usually about the ability to sell more, or sell more at a higher price. So how can you help your clients do that? This usually means that you need to understand what your client does for their customers, and help them to do it better.

Cost Reduction. Many businesses have focussed a great deal on cost reduction as a means of improving margins and profitability. As the current market situation develops it is likely that further reviews of costs will take place and, clearly, any firm that can demonstrate that they can help reduce a business's costs will be listened to seriously. However, do not confuse cost reduction with price reduction. They are not the same thing. Saving a customers' costs does not mean you have to lower your own prices.

Never confuse cost reduction with price reduction.........

If you are an existing supplier you are likely to be asked to reduce your prices, but what customers are really looking for are ways of reducing costs. Price is just the easy option. Indeed, if you can lower a customers' costs in a way that other companies have not considered or cannot do, this may be a differentiation that allows you to increase your price!

Emotional Contribution. It's amazing how many business people I see using their Mont Blanc pens and gazing at their Rolex watches. Does a Mont Blanc write better than other pens? Does a Rolex tell the time any better than any other watch? Probably not, but it does make you feel good using it or wearing it. Emotional contribution is about that and more. It's about feeling good about the people you want to do business with. It's about reducing risk and building relationships. It's about the much more subjective side of decision making. In many ways, it's the most important part of decision making. The only person who made decisions completely logically was Spock on Star Trek. So unless you're Spock it is likely that in your own decision making there is a degree (possibly a high degree) of emotion. Your clients are just the same. But to understand the emotional side of their decision making you really need to understand them deeply. However, now is not necessarily the time to rely purely on the quality of relationships. Everyone is under pressure to review costs so don't fall into the trap of over-estimating the value of the relationships you have. (but don't under estimate them either!)

As a starting point to understanding the value you offer, you need to understand all the elements of "The Value Triad©"as they apply to you and your business. However, perhaps more importantly, if you want to sell on value, then you need to understand the things that your clients see as valuable – their value drivers.

Why offer value?

Odd question I know, but why bother? First of all, customers are going to be taking a long, hard look at their suppliers as the business situation tightens and for the foreseeable future. Those they see as not offering value are likely to be in for a very hard time. The most likely pressure will be to drive down prices, and if you have nothing else to offer other than cheap prices, times are going to be tough – very.

However, if you can offer value, the true value that matches the key value drivers of your clients, then you may well be able to demonstrate that you can help in ways other than simple price reduction. If you can help them generate more revenue, reduce their costs or reduce risk (emotional contribution), then price reductions won't be necessary.

PART TWO: Building Value through Differentiation

As we have seen, when it comes to value everyone has different ideas, and what is value to one customer is something entirely different to another. It is not surprising, therefore, that for many, the value proposition is high on proposition (product

> *Many value propositions tend to be high on proposition but light on value........*

features, benefits, performance, price, etc) but light or negligible on value. What makes the difference? Really, really understanding your customer and his needs so well that we intuitively construct exactly the right deal! A good salesman often comes intuitively to the right answer. The Value Triad provides a solid basis for identifying important elements of value in any given situation, the lens through which customer needs can be more accurately analysed.

A day in the life......
When I was a very young salesman, fresh from the company's six week training course, my first week was exciting, terrifying and almost disastrous.

On the last day of the week I was confronted with what I had been dreading. The really awkward customer who, no matter what I said, had the same answer... "someone else does that, son!" After 15 minutes or so of this misery, the door out of his office and the relative safety of my sparkling, new Hillman Avenger car had become extremely attractive.

What could I say or do to win this important deal? One thought kept coming back into my mind. My sales manager, through the whole six weeks, kept saying, over and over, to all of us newbies "you are important people. You have much to share with your customers. Never forget that!"

My customer was waiting for a reply. The pressure was on. What should I say? Distantly I heard a voice saying... "I'll tell you one thing you will get when you buy from us - something you will not get from anyone else. Me!" That distant voice was mine. Did I really say that out loud? I waited for the reply expecting instantly to be propelled through the front door by my customer's size 14 brogues. Instead, after about a year gazing intently at my eager, anxious young face, he said "Good one, son. I like you and you just won the deal. But don't pull that trick again"

Back in my car, I went over in my mind what had just happened. The first thing was that I had presented a comprehensive litany of everything I could think of about my product. I knew what I wanted to say, and by golly I was going to say it. The second thing I realised was that I hadn't the faintest clue about my customers industry, his company, or him. I did no research and asked exactly zero questions. I knew all about the competitors. I could discuss the technical aspects forever. But could I relate them to the needs of a real customer, in a real company in a real industry? Not a hope. I could not come up with anything approaching a coherent proposition, much less a value proposition (and much more about Value Propositions later). I hadn't the faintest notion about what was exciting and different about my product. I just knew "we were better!"

In the absence of well structured thinking, I did what most sales people do at some point. I "winged it"! When, put on the spot, I finally came up with the only thing I could think of that was different (me!) - and my customer accepted it - I was astounded. By chance I hit on one thing that against all the odds and all the evidence seemed to matter.

I could have learned from this experience the importance of doing pre-call research. I could have learned the importance of asking questions. I could even have learned that "winging it" works. But the big lesson I learned was the lesson about differentiation. A little bit of careful research, a bit more careful thinking before this interview, and a few well considered and thoughtful questions would have revealed many points of similarity. But, much more importantly, it would have highlighted the key points of difference, some or all of which "mapped" to the customer's real needs. Here, as is so often the case, those points of valuable difference are as likely to be intangible as they are tangible.

Differentiation

So what do we mean by "differentiation"? Quite simply, it is any aspect of our total customer offer which is different from the competition and, crucially, **valued by the customer**. So it is a lot more than just a difference.

Our product or service may well be different from that of the competition but unless this difference delivers real value to the customer in a way that he can identify with

Differentiation is any aspect of our total customer offer which is different from our competitors and, crucially, is valued by the customer.

and acknowledge, then it is merely a point of difference. Nothing more. And in these straitened times we are likely to be told "I'm not paying for that".

The question for us is "what are the critical differences between us and the competition - and how does this influence the value we offer?"

A company's success in meeting their customers' requirements is based, at least in part, on the differential value of its product or service offer. If delivering value is about enhancing your customers competitive advantage, and competitive advantage is about your customer's ability to leverage his differential value, then good differentiation is all about your ability to enhance your customer's differential value better than anyone else. (you might want to read that sentence again!)

A minor, incremental difference is not a differentiation unless we can demonstrate credibly how it adds real value. A change that, for instance, makes a product easier for us to produce or the service easier to deliver, is not a differentiation. It only becomes one once it can demonstrably enhance our customer's business.

Some Routes to Differentiation
Tom Peters tells the story about Walter, a New York taxi driver. As soon as you step into Walter's cab, he says "My name is Walter. It is my job to take you where you want to go safely, as quickly as possible and on time." Then he offers you a choice of newspaper for your journey (Wall

Street Journal or USA Today). Finally he offers you a choice of radio station. He has Classical, Pop or News. And you haven't even moved yet. Walter, it is rumoured, is one of the most sought after, and the best paid, cabbies in Manhattan. People will go to his usual stand and wait only for him.

Walter is successful because he understands what his customers really want, and sets out to meet these wants in a unique manner. Anyone who has ever taken a cab ride in NYC will see immediately how Walter's service is different. The point is simply this. If you can differentiate something as mundane and prosaic as a cab ride, surely you can differentiate anything?

The complex, technology-packed products many of us sell come with a host of potential differentiators. Here are a few ideas (not by any means a comprehensive list) to think about.

Consistency

Have you ever had the experience of taking your car for a service at your local garage? The first time you go, the job is done perfectly. The car is clean, performs well and the bill is reasonable. You are delighted and resolve to use this garage as your preferred service. Next time, however, the car is returned in a dreadful state. Half the work is not done, the mechanic couldn't care less, and the bill is outrageous. The service delivery here is inconsistent. There is clearly little or no quality control in operation and so the standard of service you receive is a lottery, depending on the professionalism of the individual mechanic.

We can differentiate our service by ensuring that our customers receive sterling service, not just once but every time. Dependable, reliable service breeds dependable, reliable customers.

Convenience

A major European chemicals company carved out a large slice of the market for its specialised materials used in furniture and aerospace applications. This market is dominated by huge companies such as Hexion, Bayer and DuPont and is in large measure commoditised. The standard approach is for suppliers to ship product monthly, in hundreds of tons, and for the material to be stored in huge storage tanks on site until required. This process locks up millions of euros. The supplier delivered fortnightly, guaranteeing just-in-time. The effect was that customers could reduce the size of the storage facilities required and unlock both working capital and space for new buildings.

By enhancing the convenience to your customer of using your product or service, you can lock them in – especially if your competitors cannot copy your methods.

Customised Services

Delivery of a customised service demands deep understanding of your customer's value adding processes or production operations.

Deep understanding can only come from a proper discovery process, and may require some in-depth study of the client's business. One company, operating in the energy efficiency consultancy market, routinely undertakes a detailed site by site assessment of their clients' energy consumption. As a result of the deep understanding that results, they offer highly customised recommendations for energy cost reduction. The service provider and the client share in the cost reductions achieved through implementation of the recommendations. The client pays nothing up front for the service which is undertaken completely at the service provider's risk. Customer loyalty is assured through major cost reductions – often many hundreds of thousands of pounds – that the client could never have achieved on his own. The service is difficult to copy because the consultant has years of experience, an encyclopaedic knowledge of energy costs from all suppliers, and a robust analytical process.

By clearly and thoroughly understanding your customer's value adding processes, and pinpointing where your company's unique skills can be applied, you can create a mutual dependency which yields benefits to both client **and** *service provider.*

Combinations

A well known mobile telephone operator was exploring opportunities in the fiercely competitive US mobile phone market. This market is dominated by the big players like Sprint, Verizon and AT&T. There seemed no way in. The company set about searching for a poorly served sector and discovered it in the youth market.

The typical offer for young mobile phone users was exactly the same as for adults. No other supplier had differentiated the offer to their young customers – the standard offer being monthly contract, tied handsets, peak and off-peak call rates (which, confusingly, changed frequently) and premium priced services like internet connection. The operator, long experienced in serving the youth market in its other businesses, understood the needs of young people much better than the competitors, none of whom had made any meaningful inroads into this market.

Furthermore, they had excellent contacts in the entertainment sector which provided an opportunity to provide unique, specialist content. The operator constructed a specifically targeted youth offer. They eliminated the monthly contract (a real bone of contention), provided easy to use and easy to understand call tariffs in which customers only paid for what they used, thus eliminating monthly billing and statements which parents might see, and incorporated a host of "cool" features like music, wallpapers, ringtones and even concierge services.

A particularly popular feature was the "get out of a bad date for free" service, where a pre-arranged phone call could provide an escape excuse if a date was going badly! The operator was the first to succeed in this market.

The essence of this offer was to understand the unique needs and wants of the youth market which were not being met by incumbent suppliers. From this knowledge, the company assembled a carefully crafted package of services and features that appealed to young people, but not the adult market, using its unique contacts in the entertainment field to provide content and judiciously selected handset suppliers who could provide "funky" handsets.

We have reviewed only a handful of possible ways to differentiate your product or service. There are many, many more. However you decide to differentiate, you will need to follow these steps:

- Learn as much as you possibly can about your customer, his company, and his market. There is lots of information in the public domain and it need not take a lot of time or effort to collect it. You simply cannot know too much!

- Consider what your research says about your customer's context. Where are the sources of pain and difficulty he is suffering that no-one else seems to be addressing?

- Find ways of using your company's unique capabilities, contacts, technologies or other resources, and build them into a solution that is difficult for competitors to copy – and easy for the customer to buy!

- Build a powerful value proposition and learn how to deliver it persuasively and compellingly. (We will look at how to use value, differentiation and value based pricing in building a really compelling, professional value proposition later).

Mapping your Differentiation

Who buys a Ford Mondeo car? Lots of people. The family buyer for example, will value the space, safety, reliability, comfort, attractive appearance and features like Air Conditioning, CD Player and stereo. A car fleet manager, however, has other priorities. He is interested in boot space (for carrying samples or equipment), fuel consumption, emissions, reliability, insurance costs and residual value. There is some overlap, but the two groups of buyers have different priorities. The Ford Mondeo meets all of these users' needs. One group is willing to pay for features they do not use, because they will acquire benefits that they do appreciate.

The products and services we sell will appeal in different ways to different users – even within the same market. Perhaps even in the same company! How well we meet the requirements of a particular segment of our market – with any product or service – depends on the degree to which we understand the key priorities of customers in this segment and how carefully we have differentiated our offer to meet these priorities.

To help understand this more clearly, and also to provide you with a useful tool to measure how well your product meets your customers' real needs, let's draw a Customer Value Line.

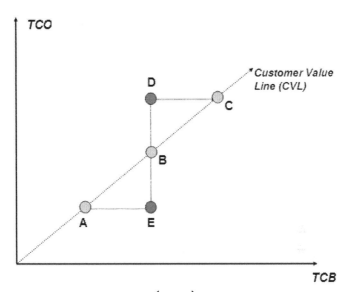

Total Cost of Ownership (TCO) is a measure of how much your product or service will cost your buyer to own and operate. TCO is more than just price. It is a combination of cost elements, some of which are incurred up-front (invoiced price, commissioning, installation, etc) and others incurred at different stages over the life of the product (training, fuel, software, repairs, etc).

Total Customer Benefits (TCB) include all the things that our customers think is important in their specific context. These include special features like output, performance etc and intangible elements such as comfort, lack of hassle, ease of use and so on. TCB and TCO vary from market to market. Even within a given market, one customer's TCO and TCB will differ from another's.

The **Customer Value Line (CVL)** represents the average relationship, for a given product and market situation, between TCO and TCB. If, like A, B and C, your product falls on the CVL, then it is delivering average (i.e. acceptable) value to your customers. If, like D, your product lies above the CVL, this represents poor customer value. For the TCO that the customer pays, he should be receiving the same TCB as the buyers of product C. He is in fact only getting the TCB of product B, which as you can see from the diagram is a lot less. Similarly, product E is a good value purchase. For the TCO of A, the customer is receiving a TCB similar to that of buyers of product B.

The suppliers of product D have a real problem. Because D offers a very poor deal, they will need to find a way of moving their product back on to, or even better, below, the CVL. The options are either to reduce TCO or to increase TCB, or some combination of the two. Often the decision is to reduce TCO (more usually to drop price). This is a bad move because it can lead to price wars and commoditisation and may also damage the perception of your brand. A much better option is to increase TCB i.e. by manipulating some elements of the TCB package that are important to the customer. These can be both tangible and intangible. Put another way, we can manipulate the Revenue Gain and Emotional Contribution elements of the Value Triad.

Let's take a completely hypothetical case of a company selling inkjet printers. Businesses which purchase ink-jet printers are looking for optimal colour quality at a low capital cost. A host of factors might influence the purchase decision, for instance, increasing revenue (from high quality colour reports or other documents), ability to link wirelessly to several PCs, reliable customer support day and night, reduced jamming, aesthetic appearance and enhancements of the buyer's business image.

Printer	Performance Scores							Weighting
Features	A	B	C	D	E	F	Average	
Text Quality	4.0	4.0	4.0	9.0	8.0	4.0	5.5	15.0
Text Speed	6.0	4.9	6.9	8.2	5.8	5.7	6.3	20.0
Graphics Quality	4.0	8.0	8.0	8.0	8.0	8.0	7.3	10.0
Ease of Use	7.0	9.0	8.0	7.0	7.0	7.0	7.5	10.0
Online help	3.0	10.0	6.0	5.0	5.0	5.0	5.7	5.0
WiFi	10.0	0.0	10.0	0.0	0.0	10.0	5.0	15.0
Paperflow	4.0	3.0	2.5	4.0	3.1	2.5	3.2	15.0
Energy Saving	10.0	10.0	10.0	8.0	4.0	8.0	8.3	10.0
TCB Score	6.2	5.2	6.8	6.1	5.0	6.2	5.9	
Cost Elements								
Capital Cost	170	100	130	150	90	150	132	
Consumables	540	352	545	370	435	572	469	
TCO Score	710	452	675	520	525	722	601	

The Table shows the TCO and TCB scores, derived from customer research, of six competitive printers, across the attributes considered important by customers in making a purchasing decision.

CVL for Inkjet Printers

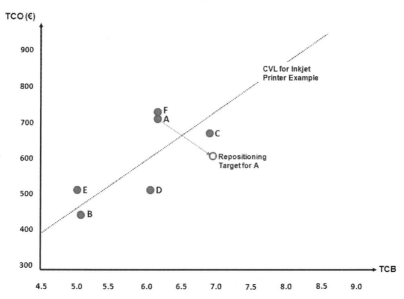

When plotted on the CVL, it becomes clear that A is positioned above the line, in a position that represents poor value. This explains why the product is not selling. Even if the PC magazines "rave" about it, the evidence from customer research, the numbers plotted into the chart, tell a quite different story! What A must do is reposition itself somewhere on or below the CVL so that it becomes a much more attractive product for purchasers. The question is – how?

We decide on the appropriate action by exploring the available options. The price may be too high. The product may be wrongly designed. Or somehow the market isn't getting the message. The first instinct is merely to drop price. This would almost certainly be completely the wrong thing to do, for the reasons described above.

A much better reaction would be to look at the product's performance in the critical user areas. Note that the customer-valued issues of text and graphics output quality, print speed and online help are well below average. So we need to boost these. The effect will be to move A to the right on the CVL.

There is a third option, which might, in panic, be overlooked. Take a cold, careful look at your promotional message. Is the message overly complex and technical (can customers actually understand and appreciate what you are saying?) You might not need to make any changes at all to the product or even the price. Creating the right marketing messages – and making sure these are consistently and professionally delivered via your sales collateral and the sales team, may just do the trick.

Of course, this case study is completely fictitious. Such a pity Product A got into this mess to begin with. Wouldn't it have been so much better to have thought through, very carefully, what customers really, really wanted, and then designed the product with the customer in mind. With that insight, we could then apply our unique capabilities as a company and deliver a highly differentiated product to the market. One that is easier to sell and represents real value to the customer in a way nobody could easily copy!

The simple, key messages from this are:

First, work really, really hard at understanding what your customers really want – what will make a difference in their world. **Secondly** use your company's unique capabilities to deliver this in a way that will create "wow!" and which cannot easily be copied. **Thirdly**, don't immediately panic and drop price if the product performs poorly. You might just need to tweak a few things – you are in a competitive market after all. Or take another look at your sales message.

> *Understand your customer.......utilise your company's unique capabilities..... and don't resort to dropping prices as the easy option!*

Never, never forget that if you don't offer real value to your customer, just being different is going to get you nowhere!

PART THREE: Building a Value-Based Price (V.B.P.)

"Okay, Dave. I'll be right there." As Jack put down the phone and made his way to No 2 building he reflected on his long and successful career as production director at the Zenith chemicals processing complex. Dave was his most recent employee (and the brightest with a brand new PhD in chemical engineering), but he still seemed quite unable to understand how this process plant worked. After checking a few dials and turning a few control valves the whole operation started up again. That same afternoon Jack was due to go to his retirement presentation. In three days his 35 years service would come to an end. At the retirement event the chief executive said: "Jack, no one knows this place like you do. If we ever have any problems, I will be sure to give you a call. Would you be willing to help?"

"Of course", Jack had said. "No problem!"

A few days later the phone rang and it was Dave again. "Jack there is a blockage in number three reactor. Can you come and sort it out?.

As Jack went through the main entrance he was met by his ex-assistant and went straight to the reactor. The CEO was already there, striding up and down impatiently.

"Jack – please! Get this @@@@ thing working again. Fast."

Jack did his usual walk up and down, looked at a few dials, tweaked a few valves and knocked on a few pipes. He made one chalk mark and told Dave that if he opened up the panel right where the chalk mark was placed, he would be able to trace the blockage, resolve it quickly and get the whole process working smoothly again.

The CEO said "Thanks Jack. Please just send in your invoice."

A day or two later the CEO was on the line, shouting down the phone.

"How on earth did you come up with $20,000? I want an itemised bill. Jack, of course, complied. His invoice showed:

For making one chalk mark	$1
For knowing where to put it	$19,999

The story might be made up but the message is very clear. What Jack possessed was a lifetime of knowledge and experience. He knew, better than anyone else, that if the production processes were to go off-line for any more than a few hours the cost to Zenith would be hundreds of thousands of dollars. Knowing just exactly where to place a chalk mark represented Jack's unique expertise - expertise which nobody else in Zenith possessed and which took decades of experience to accumulate.

This is an example of VBP.

What is VBP?

Cost-Based Pricing and Competition-Based Pricing are used in almost every company throughout Europe and the United States. These methods have been in use for decades and are familiar to most business people.

In **Cost-Based Pricing** we total up the costs to us of delivering a service or creating a product. We add on a percentage (which we call our "markup"). This creates a price. Easy and quick.

In **Competition-Based Pricing** we try to position the product in line with other similar competitive products being offered to the market at the same time and, based on specifications, make a judgement of just where the price should be pitched. If our product is a little better, we price it a little higher. If our product is not as good as the competition, we price it a little bit lower.

Most companies use both Cost- and Competition-Based approaches in making pricing decisions. The big problem, however, is that neither of these approaches captures fully the value delivered to customers. We may, just like Jack, have immense experience or unique expertise which benefit our customers. But by positioning our price at around the average in the market we would be giving away far, far too much, and giving customers a fantastic deal. Basing it on cost alone may be even worse! The problem is that we lose out in this situation - we could do so much better!

A Value Based Price is calculated on the basis of the advantages that our product or service delivers to the customer. This is the only pricing methodology that captures value and usually generates superior economic returns.

Even though this approach to pricing can, when used properly, generate much greater profits and improved customer relationships than conventional pricing methods, very few companies are yet using VBP. There are a few critical points to be aware of in VBP.

First, and vitally important, we need to be able to clearly differentiate our products or services from those of the competition. If we have no clear differentiation then we simply cannot claim superior customer value. So we cannot possibly price on customer value. If we cannot find some meaningful differentiated advantage, we run the risk of commoditisation and all the misery that goes along with it.

Secondly we need to know a great deal about the context of our customers' businesses and markets. Without this information it will be very difficult to identify relevant value or to quantify the advantages that we bring.

Thirdly, since each customer is different, our products and services will offer different advantages to each. In each case we have the opportunity to charge a different price, depending on value delivered.

How to Build a Value Based Price
In the first Chapter we introduced the concept of the Value Triad©. We use the Value Triad© as a tool, a lens through which we can analyse the real value that customers require and the value that we can offer. This may be related to reducing customers' costs, to increasing customers' productivity, to reducing hassle or to improving his peace of mind or a combination of all three. The first two elements of the Value Triad© - Revenue Gains and Cost Reductions - are generally relatively easy to quantify. It is more difficult to put an economic value on Emotional

Contribution. (That does not mean that emotional contribution is unimportant. Of course not! We use it as part of our selling argument).

There is another important element in the makeup of the VBP - the Reference Price. This is the price that the customer is accustomed to paying for a product or service similar to the one that you are offering – i.e. the Reference Product. It would be the one he would choose if your option was not available. If our product offers no added value compared to the reference product then there is neither revenue gain nor cost reduction.

Therefore we cannot use VBP. The diagram below shows how a VBP is built up from these building blocks.

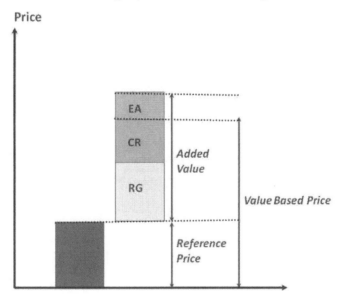

It should be obvious that we need to know quite a lot about our customers' business to be able to assess how our product or service enhances revenue streams or helps eliminate costs. However once we have this information, and we are able to justify our calculations, then it is pretty straightforward to estimate a target VBP.

Perhaps a simple (fictitious) example will make the process clearer.

A company has developed a new earth-moving machine for construction customers. The typical customer is already using a competitive machine which is coming to the end of its useful life. The replacement price is £100,000. Over its lifetime that machine generated revenue of £500,000. Fuel costs, spare parts and maintenance labour were £75,000 £35,000 and £60,000 respectively (and this is not expected to change with a re-purchase).

Our machine is built using different technology and over its life is expected to generate £750,000 in revenues. Fuel, spare parts and maintenance labour costs are £68,000, £30,000 and £34,000 respectively over the life of the equipment. The revenue gain - the additional productivity our machine offers the customer compared to the alternative - is an extra £250,000; the cost reduction is £38,000. So the total Value Based Price we can justify on the basis of superior performance and cost reduction is £388,000. We calculate this using the formula:

Maximum Value Based Price = Reference Price + Revenue Gain + Cost Reduction

	Competitor's Machine	Our Machine	Our Value Added	Comments
Price	£100,000			
Revenue	£500,000	£750,000	£250,000	Better performance leads to better productivity
Costs:				
Fuel	£75,000	£68,000	£7,000	9.3% less fuel
Spare Parts	£35,000	£30,000	£5,000	14.3% fewer spare parts
Maintenance Labour	£60,000	£34,000	£26,000	43.3% less maintenance labour
Total Added Value			£288,000	
Maximum VBP			£388,000	

Our machine is actually more robust and will last at least two years longer than the alternative. Certain aspects of product design, mostly to do with ease of access for repair and servicing, means that in case of a breakdown, spare parts are easy and quick to replace. Our new machine comes with two years supply of parts. These items could easily be costed in but to keep the calculations simple and straightforward we have ignored them. Similarly, because of this, the "hassle" factor is almost eliminated. This, too, is ignored for the purpose of this calculation but it is a strong feature of the customer testimonials prepared by the marketing team.

The Negotiation Corridor

A consistent theme in VBP is the Negotiation Corridor. The key question is this: "Will the customer purchase a new product at the maximum VBP that we can justify on objective data? Or is he more likely to choose to repurchase the same machine as before?

In fact there is no advantage to him in buying a new machine at the maximum VBP. In this case he is no better off. The negotiating corridor is created by the added value, and negotiation is required to ensure that both parties gain from the process. In other words negotiation should lead to a win-win situation – in which both parties will gain.

How high a price we are able to achieve depends on the strength of our arguments, our ability as negotiators and the ability of the buyer to negotiate against us.

Comparing Conventional and Value-Based Approaches to Pricing

In the following table we compare conventional pricing approaches (cost-based and competition based) to VBP across a number of dimensions. While it is clear that VBP can potentially offer greater advantages to the user than conventional approaches, we need to use VBP carefully. It is not a panacea and it should not be used in every situation. We certainly do not encourage the re-building of price lists using VBP exclusively. This could be very dangerous indeed!

Comparison of Conventional and VBP Methods

	Competition Based	Cost Based	Value Based
Focus	Competitors' price levels	Internal costs	Win-Win
Encourages	Pursuit of market share – not profit	Formula based approach	Cooperation, partnership and deep customer knowledge
Customer relationships	Not well developed	Not well developed	Central to all transactions
Reward for innovation	Minimal	Minimal	High and sustainable returns
Selling efforts	Transactional	Transactional	Consultancy and solutions based
Inducement to buy	Discounting	Discounting	Demonstrable economic advantages
Value capture	Limited	Limited	Complete, or as well as your salespeople can negotiate

There are occasions where we should consider using VBP:

- *New or enhanced products and services* where these offer significant improvements in two or more areas of the Value Triad©.

- *Products incorporating novel technology* which offer dramatically improved performance or significantly reduced costs-in-use.

- Products *completely new* to the world with no viable alternatives.

- Where we are introducing existing products and services into a *new geography* where again they represent a major improvements in performance compared to methods existing in that geography.

Where the customer is conditioned through usage to expect high performance at unrealistically low costs, some re-education of the customer will be necessary. We are entitled to a fair return on our hard work!

Implementation of VBP

We have recently been interviewing senior executives in major companies across Europe and the USA who have introduced, or are in the process of introducing,

VBP into their organisations. Companies in industries such as chemicals, biotechnology, professional services, agriculture, engineering products, logistics, mobile telecommunications and energy are all currently implementing VBP. Some consistent messages are coming through from those interviews.

Management Support
VBP initiatives need to be driven by top management and supported positively by all other levels of management throughout the business. The creation of value in a company is "owned" by top management and is a priority for progressive businesses. In companies where VBP has been implemented effectively, top level managers are visibly seen to be driving the process.

> *VBP must be driven by top management, communicated effectively and supported at all levels of the organisation...........*

Senior and middle management levels need to provide the necessary infrastructure and resources. For example, supporting the sales staff through the provision of technical information, cost projections and productivity data and testimonials for customers.

VBP demands a shift to Consultative Selling

VBP requires products and services to be sold consultatively rather than transactionally. In companies implementing VBP, salespeople increasingly adopt the role of consultant and try to find ways of enhancing the overall effectiveness of their customers' value creating processes. This usually requires significant sales skills development and sometimes the recruitment of new salespeople.

VBP is a Journey

Effective implementation of VBP demands that the company as a whole embraces a commitment to creating and delivering value. This may require significant changes in emphasis, attitude and even organisation and will take time to implement fully. Companies need time to make the necessary changes and adjust to them.

VBP delivers better business

VBP is not merely about improved profits, although improved profits will result from effective implementation. What VBP is about is generating better business through focusing on customers who understand and will pay for value, by defining the value that is created in objective economic terms and developing better client relationships with different executives in the client organisation. VBP leads to win-win situations. It may well mean that we need to be "choosier" about who we recruit and retain as clients. But then, if we are generating better business, we can afford to lose some of the dead wood!

In Summary......
VBP is a relatively new and attractive approach to pricing. It is the only approach that will genuinely reward us fully for the ingenuity and creativity of the people in our organisation who conceived, designed and built products and solutions for our customers. While in principle the approach to VBP is easy to understand and the numbers are relatively straightforward to calculate (if you are able to obtain robust and defensible data), the real challenges are deeper engagement in value creation and delivery at all levels in our company and, generally, a much deeper understanding of our customers' value chains.

Effective implementation of VBP is utterly dependent on professional salespeople being able to capture customers' needs in terms that allow them to build viable value propositions and to deliver them convincingly and compellingly to their customers. The reward from doing this is greater profitability, better relationships and better business. In the story at the beginning of this section, Jack was not a salesman. He just knew the real value of his years of knowledge and experience. And he had the courage to ask for what this was worth to his client. Do we?

PART FOUR: Building a Compelling Value Proposition

So far we have identified what value is and taken a look at how the value we deliver can be differentiated when compared with competitors. We have looked at the opportunities and means for creating a Value Based Price. The question now is:

"How do I communicate my differentiated value to the customer?"

The Value Proposition (V.P.) is a key tool in this communication in that it effectively provides a summary for the customer that answers the question "Why should we choose you?"

However, it needs to do much more than that if it is to demonstrate that your solution is the one that most effectively addresses the customer's requirements and delivers value that competitive offerings cannot. Don't forget that, as we have seen previously, being different on its own is not a competitive advantage. Being different in ways that the customer values is.

Here is an example. Once upon a time a father and his daughter wanted to buy a little pony. They did their research and finally chose two ponies that were absolutely perfect and, by chance, exactly the same price.

Unfortunately, they just couldn't make their minds up so they decided to go back to each of the stables for a final look and to make their choice. At the first stables, the owner was delighted to see them back and took them to see the pony "It has a wonderful temperament and is simply ideal for your young daughter", he told the father "she'll love it". None of this could the father dispute.

At the second stables the owner again took them to see the pony. Turning to the little girl he said, "I can see that you and this pony are going to get on just fine". Turning to the father he said "Look, I know these decisions can sometimes be difficult. I tell you what I'll do. Make me out a cheque for the pony today. I won't cash it, I'll just put it in the file.

Tomorrow I'll load the pony onto the lorry together with enough food and hay for a couple of weeks. If after that time you decide that the pony isn't right for your little girl, I'll come and collect it and there'll be no charge. If it is – and I'm sure it will be – then I'll cash the cheque".

So which pony do you think they bought?

So what is a Value Proposition?

Right now it seems to be a very trendy thing to have. It's one of those things that everyone seems to be talking about, although most of the examples that we have seen passed off as Value Propositions are often anything but.

Let's start by saying what they are not. A V.P. is not an advertising strap line. "We deliver great value" is not a V.P.

We've looked at loads of definitions, and stolen the best bits to come up with our own!

"A value proposition is a clear statement of the results a customer gets from using your products or services which clearly differentiates your offer from those of competitors".

The V.P. is simply a summary, a bringing together of the key reasons why the customer should choose you. There is still much work to be done in communicating to the customer that you:

- truly understand their requirements
- have solutions that would address their key business issues and needs
- have identified ways in which your solutions add real value to their business

- have calculated that value for the customer
- can demonstrate how your solutions would be delivered
- have persuasive evidence to support your ability to do so

So where does the Value Proposition come from?

There are four principle drivers:

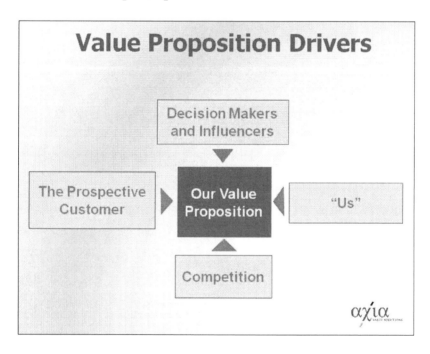

Driver 1: The Prospective Customer

This is all about understanding your customer in detail. How does your customer generate and deliver value? Do you know what their value chain looks like, who their customers are and why they buy from your prospective customer? Do you understand their market and their competitors?

Do you understand the challenges and issues that the business faces right now? Do you know their vision and long term strategy? In short, are you really interested in understanding their business?

We are frequently amazed at how little some sales people seem to know about their customers – especially since we know that one of the things that builds customer respect and trust for us is our knowledge of the customer's business.

Understanding the Prospective Customer is about building an understanding of how the functional elements of the Value Triad© - cost reduction and revenue enhancement – can be applied. What value can your solution deliver that enables the business to reduce its costs or increase its revenues (or both), and help it to more effectively add value to their own customers.

Driver 2: The Decision Makers and Influencers

Driver 1 is about understanding the business, Driver 2 is about understanding the people – businesses don't make decisions, people do. In any sales, but especially large, complex, high value sales, it is vital to know who is involved and how the decision will be made.

Again, we frequently find that whilst sellers might have identified the who, all too often there is a lack of understanding of the how. In any individual there are two primary decision driving forces at play.

Firstly, there are the functional, business objective criteria. In other words the objective business drivers behind the requirement and the decision. These may even be formalised in a specification sheet or a tender document. These are important. They are the measurable criteria against which your solution will be evaluated and compared with others

.

Secondly, however, are the individuals personal objectives, the things they want to get out of the decision. These are potentially far less easy to measure and sometimes more difficult to unearth. They are the things that are important to the individual personally. For example, if this person has only recently joined the business, and this is an important decision, they will want to make a good impression on their bosses and their peers. If they are in line for promotion, they will want to be seen to be doing a first class job.

Again, we have found that sales people, particularly the more technically driven, have difficulty breaking out of pure "functional" questioning into this more personal arena. This is a significant potential problem. It is often easy to ignore the Emotional Contribution segment of the Value Triad© and focus exclusively on the functional, objective areas of Cost Reduction and Revenue Gain. If decisions were made exclusively on the basis of logic this would be fine. However, they're not and it isn't!

Driver 3: "Us"
Driver 3 is about utilising our understanding of our own business and capabilities and matching it with the needs of the customer. Given the knowledge we have gained from our understanding of the key issues and business drivers, and from our understanding of the needs of individuals, the Value Proposition should be developed that will demonstrate our ability to address them effectively.

It must be clear by now that we firmly believe that each V.P. should be *tailored* to the specific needs of individual customers.

However, tailoring implies that something that already exists is altered to meet these needs.

We look at V.P.'s as a hierarchy:

The V.P. Hierarchy Pyramid

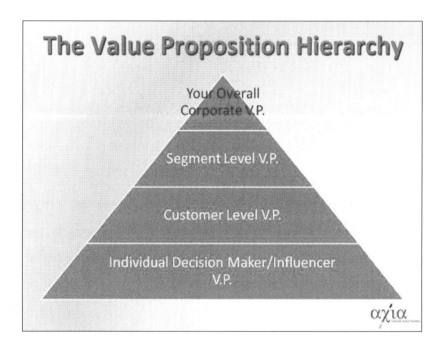

As the diagram suggests, there are a number of VP's potentially at play:

Your Overall Corporate VP: This is the overarching VP that the business communicates to its total potential market. Often this is unclear to the very people who are charged with the task of communicating it. Just ask your sales colleagues if they are clear on what the corporate value proposition is – in other words the message that they should be tailoring and communicating to their customers. If they say "yes", ask them what it is. Prepare for the silence (or the bull****).

Ideally, however, it may well be that the message in the Corporate VP is what has created the sales opportunity in the first instance.

Segment Level VP: Assuming that the business has segmented its marketplace, each segment will have a VP that is tailored to the needs of that segment. At its core will be the Corporate VP, but adapted to the segment.

Customer Level VP: The VP is tailored further to the needs of individual businesses within the segment. Again, at its core will be the corporate VP, but now targeted at the specific needs of a specific business within one of the target segments. Every business has unique problems and opportunities. It is important to identify what these are so that you can adapt your VP to demonstrate that you understand them and have ways of addressing them.

Individual Decision Maker/Influencer VP: Finally, on the basis that it is individuals that make decisions, the VP should be further tailored in conversations to the needs of these individual decision makers and influencers. The needs of the Finance Director will be different from those of the Operations Director, or those of the Managing Director and so on.

To demonstrate this, imagine that you get to the top of the Eifel Tower and discover when you get there – your one and only visit! – that you have forgotten the camera. So you ask the people with you, one to look north, one east, one south and one west, and to record in detail what they can see. Each will be seeing Paris, but each will see it from a very different perspective. The same is true in business. The FD (CFO), the MD (CEO), the OD (COO) etc. will each be seeing the same business, but from a very different perspective.

To tailor your VP, and your solutions, so that they meet the needs of individuals, you need to find out how each of them see things. "What does a good project outcome look like from your point of view?" "How do you see the situation from where you sit?"

Driver 4: The Competition

However, none of this takes place in a vacuum. Unless you are very fortunate, your proposition will be compared with that of one or more potential competitors (and don't forget that the "do nothing" option is often the most difficult competitor to overcome!)

Your VP must demonstrate that you understand their issues and have a differentiated solution that will address these issues effectively. In order to do that you must understand your competitors capabilities. This is where competitor knowledge isn't just desirable, it's essential. We often ask our delegates "what do you need to know about your competitors?" It's a one word answer – everything.

Remember, the role of the VP is to answer for the customer the question "Why should we choose you rather than one of your competitors?"

As a result, the generation of a Value Proposition is an iterative process. As your knowledge builds the VP will be, or should be, constantly finessed and refined. It should be tested out in the meetings you have with various members of the customer's team until it is honed to your best ability.

Finally, you have a Value Proposition that has been developed over time and following a detailed understanding of the elements we have identified. Ultimately it should pass:

The VP Reality Check

1. If you gave your VP to a competitor, could they use it? In other words, if they took your name off the VP and they put theirs in its place, would it still be valid. If it is, then you have not managed to create a differentiated value proposition.

2. Does it address the key issues that you have identified the customer faces? If it doesn't what does it do?

3. Can you deliver? Odd question, but you wouldn't be the first company to win business and get back to the office wondering how on earth you can do it!

The Value Proposition is much more than a current fad. Customers have increasing choice, and increasing difficulty in making informed choices – despite the mountain of information that is now available to them. A well crafted Value Proposition demonstrates that you have understood the customer and their issues, have got a solution that delivers more of the things the customer wants than competitors (it's differentiated in ways the customer values), and it makes it that little bit easier for them to make the decision – in your favour.

A Final Summary

I think every book of this type should have a summary, and here's ours, kindly provided by our great friend and colleague, Jack Matton, erstwhile member of Alstom Power, with whom we have worked all over the world. Jack provides our American perspective and, hopefully, inspires legions of American readers! It seems appropriate to leave the last few words to him......

"First you must understand your customer and what is important (valuable) to him personally and to his business in terms of the three elements of the Value Triad©.

Second you must understand your competition and how you are different from them on those issues that are important to the customer.

Third you have to quantify the monetary and emotional value (both positive and negative) of these differentiators.

Finally you have to construct a Value Proposition that clearly explains the differentiated value that your product or service brings to the customer.

At the end of the day, customers will only buy your product or service if they understand the value that you offer and they feel they have a reasonable chance of receiving that value if they purchase.

OK, a final, final thought!......Value Selling is not just an activity for the Sales Department. Value Selling is not just a fancy consultative sales process. Value Selling requires the input and support of the entire company".

Don't forget, we'd love to hear from you with your thoughts and feedback. We also run in-company workshops on value, value selling and value based pricing throughout the world.

In addition, both Mike and Harry deliver keynote addresses and boardroom briefings on the various aspects of value and value based pricing.

Please get in touch with us to discuss your requirements for workshops, consultancy or speaking engagements. info@axiavalue.com

Great value selling and profitable value pricing!

Mike Wilkinson & Harry Macdivitt

Lightning Source UK Ltd.
Milton Keynes UK
03 September 2010

159342UK00002BA/2/P